To:

My favorite sister, Judy
(February 14, 2001

Love,

Bonnie

You're such a blessing
to me!

A Special Gift

for my sister:

_____

from:

_____

date:

_____

Stories, sayings, and Scriptures to Encourage and Inspire...

hugs™

for *Sisters*

HOWARD
PUBLISHING CO.

PHILIS BOULTINGHOUSE

Personalized Scriptures by
LEANN WEISS

Our purpose at Howard Publishing is to:

- *Increase faith* in the hearts of growing Christians
- *Inspire holiness* in the lives of believers
- *Instill hope* in the hearts of struggling people everywhere

Because He's coming again!

Hugs for Sisters © 2000 by Philis Boultinghouse
All rights reserved. Printed in the United States of America
Published by Howard Publishing Co., Inc.,
3117 North 7th Street, West Monroe, LA 71291-2227

01 02 03 04 05 06 07 08 09   10 9 8 7 6 5

Personalized scriptures by LeAnn Weiss, owner of Encouragement Company,
3006 Brandywine Dr., Orlando, FL 32806; 407-898-4410

Interior design by LinDee Loveland

Library of Congress Cataloging-in-Publication Data
Boultinghouse, Philis, 1951-
    Hugs for sisters : stories, sayings, and scriptures to encourage and inspire / Philis
Boultinghouse ; personalized scriptures by LeAnn Weiss.
        p. cm.
    ISBN 1-58229-095-4
    1. Christian women—Prayer-books and devotions—English. 2. Sisters—Prayer-
books and devotions—English. I. Weiss, LeAnn. II. Title.
    BV4844 .B68 2000
    242'.643—dc21   99-059673

A special thanks to Jim McGuiggan and Mary Owen for sharing events from their
lives for story ideas for "We Shall Not Be Moved" and "Full Circle."

Scripture quotations not otherwise marked are from the The Holy Bible, New International Version (NIV). Copyright © 1973, 1978, 1984. International Bible Society.
Used by permission of Zondervan Bible Publishers. Scripture quotations marked NLT
are taken from the *Holy Bible*, New Living Translation, copyright © 1996. Used by permission of Tyndale House Publishers, Inc., Wheaton, Illinois 60189. All rights
reserved.

contents

a Sister's
perspective

*L*et your soul be at rest once more. I've been good to you…delivering your soul from death and your eyes from tears. May you walk before Me in the land of the living. My supernatural peace, which transcends all human understanding, will guard your heart and your mind.

Peacefully,
Your Father of Life

—from Psalm 116:7–9; Philippians 4:7

Sisters. There's something about the bond of sisterhood that is unlike all other unions. There's the shared femaleness—that alone is significant, but there's so much more. There's the unreasoning bond of heritage—you're bound together just because of who you are. And there's the unrelenting bond of shared experiences —you've shared secrets and Barbie dolls, Christmas mornings and roller skates. And then there's the inexplicable bond of shared genes and genetic codes that make it so much fun to say, "You look just like Mama Lou when you say that!" or "Your lasagna tastes *exactly* like Mom's!"

But this bond, this sameness, has a strange way of bringing our differences into sharp focus. And sometimes we can learn qualities or perspectives from our sisters that we do not naturally possess.

Take Mary and Martha, for instance. When Jesus came to their home, each approached her honored guest through her own distinct personality. Martha, the gracious hostess, took her responsibilities very seriously. She cooked and cleaned and fussed and fixed.

Mary, on the other hand, took *Jesus* seriously. Everything else could wait. All other responsibilities were put on hold. The Lord was in their house, and she wanted to hear every word He had to say.

On that day, Martha learned from Mary that, really, "only one thing is needed" (Luke 10:42). On another day, Mary may have learned from Martha the value of a job well done.

Sisterhood provides a safe place to learn new ideas, to explore different ways of looking at life. The comfort of our sameness helps us relax enough to learn from our differences.

So get comfortable. Put your feet up. Spend some time reflecting on the blessings of being a sister. You'll be glad you did.

When all the dust is settled
and all the crowds are gone,
the things that matter are
faith, family, and friends.

—Barbara Bush

*Their love
was rooted
in who they
were: They
were sisters.*

peace like a river

She didn't know why they had come. But here they stood, under the trees. Three sisters, side by side, arms around each other's waists. They were here to visit their brother's grave.

It had been a little more than three years since Paul had died, but when people asked Michele, the oldest of the three sisters, about her siblings, she still spoke of Paul in the present: "I have three brothers and two sisters," she'd say. She firmly believed that Paul was still very much alive—just not here.

When her younger sister Katherine, had suggested they visit his grave, Michele had hesitated. She'd always had a hard time understanding why people went to visit graves—

especially people of faith who believed that their loved ones were with God. The person was not there. Why attach such sentiment to a grave?

"Come on, Michele," her youngest sister, Mattilyn, had coaxed, "just come so we can be together."

Michele had reluctantly agreed to go.

She loved being with her sisters. She always felt an unexplainable joy and sense of completion just being with them. No three women could be more different. Mattilyn had the air of a businesswoman—always organizing, always planning. She gave financial advice to all her siblings and even took care of the accounting for their father's business. Katherine was the maternal homemaker. Baking bread, going to yardsales, and refinishing furniture were some of her favorite pastimes. Easygoing and completely candid, she liked nothing more than long conversations of honest sharing. Michele's demeanor was somewhere between Mattilyn's efficiency and Katherine's candor. She loved learning and being outdoors and spent way too many hours indoors at work. But the bond between them did not require common interests or similar personalities. Their bond was based on a shared heritage and a sense of family. Their love was rooted in who they were: They were sisters.

Their busy chatter on the way to the cemetery had jumped from their relationships with their husbands, to their children's activities, to the demands of work, to experiences at church. It was wonderful to share the day-to-day aspects of their lives in an atmosphere of complete trust and love.

When they arrived at the cemetery, Mattilyn knew just where the gravesite was. As they walked around other tombstones on the way to their brother's, their mood quieted. And now the three of them stood together, sharing unspoken feelings, uniting their spirits.

Michele remembered the morning she'd gotten the call and the heaviness in their mother's voice. "Paul's had a heart attack," their mother had said. "He died before he got to the hospital."

Michele had sat in a stupor on the side of the bed, eyes staring straight ahead, mouth hanging open, receiver dangling in her hand. Her hurriedly thrown-on robe was still unbuttoned. Tears streamed down her face. She just sat. No thoughts formed. No emotions took shape. She had been aware only of the pain.

She remembered standing in front of Paul's open coffin at the funeral home with her two sisters—in the same pose they now maintained. Loud sobs had threatened to spill from her mouth. Instead, the three women had cried quietly together. The song the congregation had sung at the church memorial service the previous night had played in her head: "When peace like a river attendeth my way, when sorrows like sea billows roll; whatever my lot, Thou hast taught me to say, 'It is well, it is well with my soul.'" It had been her brother's favorite song. He'd even rewritten the words into simple, contemporary language, and a copy of his rendition hung on Michele's den wall. As she'd looked down upon his stiff, cold body, she'd realized that her brother's death brought their family's faith into sharp focus: *So this is what my faith is all about,* she'd thought. *If I believe what I've professed to believe all my life, then I know that Paul will be raised someday, and we'll all be with him again. If that isn't true, then none of what I believe is true.* But Michele knew that it was.

And now they stood together at his grave, the truth of his absence made fresh again. And with the truth, the pain.

"Remember the time…" Mattilyn began, and for the next several minutes they shared stories of their childhood and growing up together. They laughed a little, cried some, then fell silent as each rummaged through her own treasure box of memories.

The hot sun filtered through the summer green leaves above them. A gentle breeze mercifully cooled their faces. The only sounds were the cars on the distant freeway. Each woman was absorbed in her own thoughts. Sadness began to clutch at Michele's heart. She wished they had not come. This place made her think only of death and separation. She was about to insist that they leave when a scratchy song rose up through the silence.

"When peace like a river..."

Michele was roused from her brooding.

"...attendeth my way," the voice continued.

It was Katherine. She was singing Paul's song. Her voice was weak and filled with tears, but she sang on.

"When sorrows like sea billows roll...," Mattilyn joined in.

Michele heard her own voice join the others, and all three sang haltingly in unison, "Whatever my lot, Thou hast taught me to say, 'It is well, it is well with my soul.'"

At that moment, no force could have pulled the three sisters apart. Clinging to each other for support, their voices gained strength as they sang on, "And, Lord, haste the day when the faith shall be sight, the clouds be rolled back as a scroll, the trump shall resound and the Lord shall descend, even so, it is well with my soul."

a *Sister's* perspective

As their song concluded, a vague understanding began to come over Michele. At first, she didn't recognize what it was. But her emotions took form, and she began to understand why it was good that they had come. They had come to share memories of someone they loved; they had come to be reminded of their eternal hope. They had come to honor their brother Paul. Not because they thought that in some sense he was still there, but because they knew *Whose* he was and *where* he was. Maybe he was even looking down on them right now. Maybe he was even singing with them.

She closed her eyes, and she could see his face. She saw the mischievous twinkle in his eyes and his easy, gentle smile. She heard his sweet voice. And with the memory came a wonderful sensation. She felt it go all through her. Slow...cool...calm. She took a deep breath, and the feeling intensified—refreshing her tired heart, soothing her soul. It flooded her body, almost in a physical sense, and filled her with an all-consuming sense of well-being. Then she knew what it was. It was peace—the peace that Paul had loved to sing about—the peace that must accompany him now. Peace.

Peace...like a river.

She was glad they had come.

2

a Sister's love

$\mathscr{H}$ow great is My love I've lavished on you that you should be called My child. You can love because I first loved you. True love isn't envious or boastful. It always protects, always hopes, always perseveres, and never fails.

My Everlasting Love,
Your God of Love

—from 1 John 3:1; 4:19; 1 Corinthians 13:4, 7–8

Sisters

Sisters are connected at the very deepest levels. Either she was there when you were born, or you were there when she was. Either way, you've been together from the very start.

She knows about the time you told Mom and Dad that you were studying at the library with a friend… You know about the time she spent all her Christmas money on one concert ticket. She knows what makes you tick, and you know what ticks her off.

Such intimate knowledge carries with it great power—potentially dangerous power. But when coupled with love, it's one of the strongest forces for good in the universe.

The source of this vast power is the Creator of sisters. His unquenchable love is described in the Book of Romans: "Nothing can ever separate us from his love…. Our fears for today, our worries about tomorrow, and even the powers of hell can't keep God's love away. Whether we are high above the sky or in the deepest ocean, nothing in all creation will ever be able to separate us from the love of God that is revealed in Christ Jesus our Lord" (8:38–39 NLT).

The love we learn from God has the power to hold sisters together in the face of *anything*. The love of a sister can fly across an ocean in a letter and fill a lonely heart with joy; it can travel through telephone wires to bring courage to a weary soul; it can pierce a hardened heart and infuse it with hope; why, it can even be perceived by an unborn child in her mother's womb.

Nothing can separate those bound by the power of love.

*Those who bring sunshine
to the lives of others cannot
keep it from themselves.*

—James M. Barrie

"You'll never know, dear,
How much I love you.
Please don't take
My sunshine away."

you are my sunshine

"Mommy, when is baby Mary going to come out of your tummy?" Crystal asked for the hundredth time that day.

"In just a few more days," Sue assured her. "Come here, feel my tummy. Can you feel her kicking? That's Mary's way of saying, 'I'll be there soon, big sister; I'll be there soon.'"

Four-year-old Crystal moved her face closer to her mother's rounded belly. "You are my sunshine, my only sunshine," she sang in sweet, soothing tones. "You make me happy when skies are gray…"

The song had become a tradition. When Sue and her husband, Rob, had first told Crystal about the coming baby and that she would share Crystal's room, Crystal had put her hands on her hips, stuck out her lip, and said, "I don't want to share my room with a ba-a-aby!" She'd drawn out the first syllable and infused every ounce of disgust into the word that a four-year-old could muster. "It will cry and break my toys and lose all my baby dolls!"

"Why, Crystal," Sue had crooned, "that's no way for a big sister to talk!"

Crystal's defiant pout had turned to wide-eyed surprise in an instant. "What do you mean, 'sister'?"

Crystal knew all about sisters. Her best friend from pre-school, Jennifer, was a sister. She was a "big" sister at that. Jennifer's new baby sister wore pink, frilly dresses and giggled and grinned when Jennifer said her name. And Crystal's mom had two sisters. When Aunt Lesa and Aunt Ruth came over for lunch, they'd sit at the table with Mommy—their heads close together, laughing and talking. One day, Aunt Ruth had laughed so hard she'd fallen out of her chair.

"Okay," Crystal had conceded, "you can have a baby, and I'll be a big sister." The matter was settled.

The next day, Crystal had trotted into the kitchen where Sue was peeling potatoes. "Mommy," she began hesitantly, "I've been thinking."

"Oh, you have, have you?"

"Yes. I've been thinking that our baby needs a song. I have a song, and baby Mary needs a song too."

"Yes, you do have a song," said Sue as she scooped Crystal into her arms and began to sing, "You are my sunshine, my only sunshine…"

Crystal sang the next line, "You make me happy when skies are gray."

They finished in duet, "You'll never know, dear, how much I love you; please don't take my sunshine away!"

At the conclusion of the song, Crystal laughed with glee and hugged Sue tight. But as she pulled away from her hug, Crystal's face turned somber. "Mommy, am I still your sunshine? Or is baby Mary going to be your new sunshine?"

Sensing the importance of the moment, Sue sat down in the big rocking chair and pulled Crystal close. "No one will ever take your place, my little sunshine. 'You make me happy when skies are gray!' That song is just for you. We'll find a different song for baby Mary."

Crystal seemed satisfied and lay her head against her mother's chest in a rare moment of stillness. No sooner had she gotten settled than she jerked up again, her eyes shining with excitement. "I know what, Mommy! I'll be *your* sunshine, and baby Mary can be *my* sunshine!" With that, she slid out of Sue's lap and stood on the floor between her mother's legs. Bringing her little face up close to Sue's abdomen, she began to sing, "You are my sunshine, my only sunshine. You make me happy when skies are gray…"

And so it was. At least once a day, every day, for the next six months, Crystal would take time out of her busy play to sing to her baby sister, who was growing safe and warm in their mother's womb.

Summer turned to fall, and one night, just before Thanksgiving, Sue was awakened by contractions that were undeniably the real thing. Everything had been planned. Ruth was at their house in just minutes to stay with Crystal. Lesa would meet them at the hospital. Rob called the doctor and the hospital. Sue's bags were packed, and the car was facing the street.

As Rob and Sue drove the two miles to Memorial Hospital, Sue handled her contractions with practiced ease. One big, cleansing breath in…blow it out; then, in through the nose, out through the mouth, until the contraction was over. When they got to the hospital, Lesa greeted them at the door, and the nurse was waiting for them with a wheelchair. In the birthing room, Sue settled into the crisp, clean sheets and tried to focus on her focal point as the next contraction rolled over her. They were coming in earnest now, and it took all her concentration to keep her breathing in rhythm. But as each contraction concluded, Rob encouraged her and assured her that she was doing fine.

And for the next few hours, everything was fine.

Until Sue caught a glimpse of the nurse's face as she watched the green line on the screen that represented baby Mary's heartbeat. Sue couldn't see the screen, but she could see the nurse's furrowed brow. And it said more than the nurse intended.

"What's wrong!" Sue demanded, but the nurse scurried out of the room without answering.

Fear rose in Sue's throat, and as the next contraction began, she was unable to catch her breath and she lost control. She tightened her hold on Rob's hand, and as the contraction peaked, she let out her first scream.

"It's okay, Sue," Rob soothed, "you'll get back in rhythm on the next one."

"No," Sue moaned, "there's something wrong. I saw it in the nurse's eyes. There's something wrong with our baby!"

"I'm sure everything is fine," Rob insisted. "You were just imagining it."

But there was no time for Sue to protest. The next contraction came without warning, and with it came an engulfing panic. Sue's scream filled the room.

Her doctor burst into the room, and three nurses followed close behind, dragging a table filled with glistening instruments.

"Mrs. Gibbs," her doctor began, "your baby's heartbeat is not what it should be. We need to take the baby by C-section."

Sue's eyes filled with fear, and her mind filled with questions. But the only thing that came out of her mouth was, "Whatever you need to do, doctor, just take care of my baby."

The nurse injected something into her I.V., and within minutes, she felt her eyelids growing heavy and her body relaxing. She began to drift...

Sue awoke with an overwhelming sense of doom. Trying to sort through the fog in her mind, she struggled to open her eyes. They refused to cooperate. Suddenly she remembered, and her eyes popped open of their own accord. Her baby! What had happened to her baby? The first face she saw was that of her older sister, Lesa. She shifted her gaze, and Rob came into focus.

It took all her effort, but she finally formed the only question that mattered: "Is she alive? Is my baby alive?"

Rob squeezed her hand, "Yes, Sue, she's alive. But..." His voice trailed off; he could not finish.

"She's in trouble, Sue," Lesa said steadily. "She's breathing, but she's not conscious. The doctors don't know if she'll make it."

Over the next several days, Sue would not leave the side of the tiny bassinet in the pediatric ICU unit. She cried, she prayed, and she waited. But little Mary lay listless and unmoving.

Each day that brought no change diminished little Mary's chance of survival. Finally, Sue was told that her little one would not survive the coming night.

Her thoughts turned to Crystal. How would they help her understand? Crystal so wanted to be a big sister. "Nurse," Sue said, "I want my daughter Crystal to see her little sister before she dies."

"I'm sorry, Mrs. Gibbs, but children aren't allowed in this unit. There's too much danger of infection to the other babies. There's just no way."

From some inner source, a fierce strength welled up in

Sue, and her eyes blazed with purpose. "My child *will* see her sister," she affirmed.

Within the hour, Sue had spoken to the administrator and Crystal was standing beside her tiny sister's bassinet. She'd brought her favorite baby doll, and she placed it gently among the tubes that monitored and fed little Mary.

Rob and Sue clung to each other as they watched their two little girls. The only sound was the incessant beeping of the machines that surrounded their precious, dying child. Then, over the beeping came the sweet voice of little Crystal.

"You are my sunshine, my only sunshine…"

Sue struggled to silence the sob that threatened to fill the room and break the spell.

"You make me happy when skies are gray…"

As Crystal continued to sing, Sue fixed her gaze on the tiny figure in the tangle of tubes. Suddenly, she thought she saw Mary's little finger move. Surely she was mistaken. She watched intently, not taking her eyes off the tiny fingers.

"You'll never know, dear…"

Yes, she was sure of it now. Mary's fingers were moving. Rob saw it too.

"How much I love you…"

The nurse came in and saw it too. The three adults stood transfixed.

"Please don't take my sunshine away."

When Crystal finished her song, the nurse moved swiftly to her side. "Don't stop singing, honey. Sing your song again. Your little sister likes to hear you sing."

Over the following days, Crystal visited often and sang her sister's song. The tender melody had penetrated the walls of the womb as little Mary had grown inside her mother's body, and now the familiar, soothing tones of the simple song brought her out of the coma and into the world of baby dolls and big sisters.

And as the years passed and the sisters grew, it was not unusual to see them swinging in tandem in the backyard as their sweet, tender voices drifted through the air: "You'll never know, dear, how much I love you; please don't take my sunshine away."

3

a *Sister's*
comfort

$\mathcal{I}$ am close to you when you are brokenhearted and crushed in spirit. Cast all of your worries upon Me, because I care for you. I, even I, am He who comforts you. I'll exchange your sorrow for comfort and joy.

Love,
Your God of All Comfort

—from Psalm 34:18; 1 Peter 5:7; Isaiah 51:12; Jeremiah 31:13

Sisters

A sister, it seems, has extrasensory perception. When you hurt, she feels your pain. When you're happy, she shares your joy. When you're frightened, she understands.

And when a dark day comes, a sister's not afraid to enter into the darkness with you. She walks in—invited or not, it doesn't matter—and she brings with her the comfort of God. What she's really bringing is *recycled* comfort.

Second Corinthians tells us that God "comforts us in our troubles, so that we can comfort those in any trouble with the comfort we ourselves received from God" (1:4).

The comfort God offers us when we're hurting is recycled and used to comfort the hurting heart of another. That's what a sister brings with her when she walks into your darkness. She brings the comfort of God recycled just for you.

And a sister has a special advantage when it comes to the comfort ministry. She can hear the hidden fear in your voice that no one else can hear. She can see the masked sadness on your face that no one else can see. Even when you try to hide your worry or your pain, a sister can often see through you, right to the truth.

And aren't you glad she can? Although she drove you crazy when you were ten—and still does on occasion—her keen perception sees who you really are, and she loves you anyway.

A sister who can do that—who can see straight through to the truth of you, who can be *trusted* with the truth of you—is like a "ministering angel" (Hebrews 1:14) sent straight from heaven to you with a recycled hug of comfort.

There never was a heart truly great and generous that was not also tender and compassionate.

—Robert Frost

There was something
about that old blanket
that conjured up
feelings of security,
love, and comfort.

blue Monday

It was Saturday morning, and she'd awakened to an empty bed once again. When Sarah had finally fallen into a fitful sleep the night before, her husband, Jake, had not been home. He hadn't called to say he'd be late, he hadn't made an excuse before leaving for work in the morning—he just hadn't come home.

They'd had an argument the day before, but she knew that wasn't the reason he hadn't come home. They argued all the time these days. And never about anything she could put her finger on.

Over the last few weeks, Sarah's emotions had run the whole gamut. She'd felt fear, anger, strength, weakness, betrayal, hope, and desperation. She'd felt it all. What she felt most of all now was tired.

She hadn't told anyone about her growing fear or her suspicions about Jake's whereabouts. Not her friends, not her parents, not even her sister Liana. Liana was so strong, and her relationship with her husband, Jim, was so loving. Liana would be so disappointed in Sarah if her marriage unraveled. They all would. She had to keep it together. Somehow. She had to.

As she turned her face to her pillow, her thoughts went unwittingly to the old, blue blanket she'd had as a child. There was something about that old blanket that conjured up feelings of security, love, and comfort…feelings that her life was totally lacking these days.

Her mind drifted, and she recalled the story her father had told her a hundred times. A story that she loved to hear even now. When her mother found out that she was pregnant with Sarah, her Grandma Jo had knitted her a special blanket. That blanket went with her mother to the hospital with explicit instructions to "wrap that baby up in this blanket when you bring her home." It was a blue blanket with fringed ends. Grandma Jo had made Liana one just like it when she'd been born just fourteen months earlier.

Those blankets were constant companions to the insep-
arable sisters. They transformed magically into all sorts of
things: silk shawls for make-believe parties, superhero capes
for flying off the dining-room table, and magic cloths for
revealing secret mysteries. But most of all, they were comfy
blankets. When she and Liana were little, they would
snuggle under their blankets in front of the TV on Saturday
mornings, stick their thumbs in their mouths, and watch
their favorite cartoons together. When a scary noise came
from the hall as they were trying to fall asleep at night,
they'd pull their blankets over their heads and squeal for
Mom and Dad to come save them. And when they got older
and went away to camp, they tucked their blankets into
their sleeping bags for a little touch of home. They even
took their blankets with them to their shared dorm room in
college and draped them over their matching bedspreads—
for that "homey look," they said.

And now, from somewhere far in her past, her heart cried
out for her comfy blanket. But Sarah's blanket had been lost
on a cruise that she and Jake had taken two years earlier.
That cruise was the last time they had enjoyed a really good
time together. When she'd unpacked her bags, the blanket
was not there. She'd called the cruise line, but they couldn't

find it. *No matter,* Sarah had thought. *It's just a silly old blanket.* But deep down, she knew it was more.

Sarah was jolted from her musings by the slamming of the door. Jake was home. Sarah couldn't decide if she should jump out of bed and demand to know where he'd been or retreat under the covers and pretend she was asleep. She didn't have to think about it for long.

"I'm leaving," he said, as he walked decidedly into their bedroom. He stood at the foot of the bed, feet squared, jaw clenched. She could tell he'd practiced what he was about to say. "I want a divorce. I don't love you anymore, and I don't think I can love you again. I've found someone I do love. We've decided to get married. I hope you won't give me any trouble."

Sarah slowly sat up in bed. It was impossible to absorb the impact of his words. She knew things weren't good between them, but she'd just assumed that they would get better.

How could this be happening to *her?* From the time she and Liana were little girls, they'd talked about what their lives would be like when they married. She loved the idea of marriage. She even loved Jake. She and Jake were active in their church. At least she was—and he used to be.

She tried to think of words that would make him stay, that would change his mind, but her thoughts would not form. Words refused to come together.

It didn't matter. She didn't need to say anything. Jake was already on his way out the door. He had just walked in, made his announcement, and walked out. She heard the front door slam again. He was gone.

Panic rose in her throat. She could feel it as a tangible lump. It was cutting off her air. Her heart was pounding so hard she could hear it thudding in her ears. Sarah felt as if she were on the verge of something dangerous. This was the closest she'd ever come to "cracking up." She jumped out of bed and paced frantically back and forth in front of the phone, trying to decide what to do. She should call someone. Do something. But *what? Who?* She was too ashamed. She felt like an absolute failure. And she was so tired—so sick of it all—so bewildered.

And then the tears began to flow. They welled up from her abdomen with a growing strength and venom. They consumed her body, and she began to shake from the force of her weeping. She thought that surely her insides would come out and she would simply die.

She felt her knees buckle, and she fell to the floor. She

was overcome with a conviction that she had taken all she could take. She couldn't take any more. If relief didn't come, she would simply disintegrate—there wouldn't be anything left of her.

That's when the phone rang—as she lay crumpled on the floor, right before she disintegrated into nothingness. She pushed herself up to her knees, then pulled herself up to the nightstand. It must be Jake. He would tell her he was sorry. He was coming home. He really did love her after all.

Her hands were shaking as she reached for the receiver. She tried to gain control of her voice.

"Hello," she said expectantly.

"Sarah? Is that you?"

It wasn't Jake. It was her sister Liana.

Sarah didn't mean to tell her, but the words just tumbled out. She'd kept everything in so long and was so full of pain that when she heard the sound of a loving, familiar voice, the pain flowed out of her mouth, and she told it all.

The telling left her even more exhausted, but she also felt some relief. Liana's soothing voice held no hint of condemnation, no suggestion of disappointment. Only acceptance. Only comfort. Only steadfast love.

By the time Sarah hung up the phone, she knew that

somehow she would make it. She didn't know how, but some small part of her believed that by God's power, she would not disintegrate. Somehow she would live.

She managed to fake it through the weekend by sheer force of will. She got her two children where they needed to be on Saturday, and she somehow went through the motions of going to church on Sunday. But as soon as she got Jason and Jacob off to school Monday morning, she collapsed on the couch. All the tears she'd hidden while her children were home came pouring out now that she was alone. The pain of it all hit her afresh. Her chest hurt. Her eyes ached.

She didn't know how long she'd sat in her trancelike stupor before she heard her doorbell ring. She made a semi-effort to wipe the tears and rivers of mascara from her face as she shuffled to the door. She was surprised to see a postal worker standing there.

"Good morning, ma'am. I've got a package for you," he said as he thrust a blue and white box at her. "Please sign here."

Sarah mechanically signed her name, took the package, and closed the door.

She couldn't imagine what the package held. She

opened the end of the box. She pulled out a bundle wrapped in blue tissue paper. It was a blanket. For a brief second she thought that maybe the people from the cruise line had finally found her long-lost comfy blanket. But then she saw the card, written in Liana's familiar script.

> *I know you're running a little short on comfort right now, so I thought I'd lend you mine.*
>
> Your sister forever,
>
> Liana

Sarah tenderly lifted the worn, faded blanket to her face. She closed her eyes, and she was little again—snuggled up on the couch with Liana, whispering secrets that only they shared, and eating warm chocolate-chip cookies straight from the oven. She took a deep breath and was filled with memories of spring days outside and running with magic capes flying behind them in the wind.

A warmth and assurance that she hadn't felt in months oozed through her. From somewhere deep inside an awareness began to dawn. A faint ray of hope. From miles away, her sister's love comforted her and filled her with the promise of future joy.

blue Monday

She wasn't strong now, but with the Lord's help and the comfort of her faithful sister, she would find her strength again.

4

a *Sister's*

support

$\mathcal{I}$ have redeemed you, calling you specifically by name. From the fullness of My grace, you have received one blessing after another. My plans stand firm forever, the purposes of my heart through all generations.

Victoriously,
Your Heavenly Father

—from Isaiah 43:1; John 1:16; Psalm 33:11

Sisters

How is it that there's so much strength in your sister's hand?

When you were little, walking down a long, dark hall by yourself was unthinkable. But with your sister's hand wrapped around yours, you found the strength to do together what you could not do alone.

Even now, when she places her hand in yours, her strength enables you to make it through the tough times. When you anxiously await the test results...when you're feeling frazzled and undone...when you stand before the coffin of a loved one...when you think you can't make it through another day...when your kids are giving you fits...when you're having a very bad hair day...

When her hand takes yours, the strength and fortitude that hold her together flow from her and into you. You can

almost feel it physically; you can certainly
feel it in your heart. You can breathe again.
Your frantic heart slows its pace, your frenzied
mind regains its composure, and your drifting
spirit finds its anchor.

When sisters share their strength with each
other—and like Jesus, stand by our sides and give us
strength (2 Timothy 4:17)—they do more than
share their own strength; they share the strength of
the Lord.

When you stand at your sister's side and share
your strength with her, you allow God to work
through you to share the strength He has
placed in your heart.

When she slips her hand into yours—
while life's troubles may not melt away
—you feel a surge of strength and a
lightening of the load. Reach
out…let the strength of the
Lord flow between you.

For when three sisters love each other with such sincere affection, the one does not experience sorrow, pain, or affliction of any kind, but the others' heart wishes to relieve, and vibrates in tenderness. Like a well-organized musical instrument.

—Elizabeth Shaw

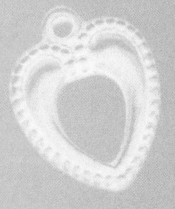

Her sister's voice flew through the telephone wires, bristling with excitement. "It's him; I just know it!"

full circle

The harsh ringing jerked Jo Ann out of a sound sleep. As she rolled over and reached for the phone, the bright red numbers on her alarm clock told her it was 1:47 A.M. Myriad worries flashed through her mind in a brief second. Were her girls okay? Yes, she'd checked on them just before she'd gone to bed, and they were all tucked in and sleeping cozily. John! Had John had an accident? No. Her husband lay soundly sleeping by her side. Oh, no. Her father was in the hospital with pneumonia. That must be it. He must have taken a turn for the worse. She braced herself for bad news as she picked up the receiver.

"Jo Ann!" came the hushed voice on the other end of the line.

"Maxine, is that you?" Jo Ann whispered. "What's wrong? Is Daddy okay?"

"Daddy's fine. Everything's fine!" Maxine's voice was breathless with excitement. Jo Ann knew her sister well enough to know that she was bursting with a secret.

"You'll never guess where I am!" Maxine whispered.

"Speak up, Maxine, I can barely hear you. What on earth is going on?"

"I can't talk any louder. I don't want anyone to hear me. You have to guess! Guess where I am!"

Jo Ann didn't feel like playing games, but she knew her sister wouldn't give up the secret without at least a little effort on her part. Jo Ann searched her mind. She knew Maxine had gone on a church trip to a small town in South Carolina that had been hit by a devastating tornado. Members of the church whose homes had not been damaged were housing the relief crew.

"Oh, Maxine…" she tried to keep the irritation out of her voice, "I know you're in Charleston, but what's so exciting about that?"

full circle

"It's not the city I'm in that's so incredible; it's whose *house* I'm in—whose *room* I'm in!"

Maxine was a history buff. She loved the Old South and all the romantic tales like *Gone with the Wind*. "Are you in some old plantation home?" Jo Ann guessed. "Is that what you woke me up in the middle of the night to tell me?"

John rolled over and almost woke up. Jo Ann eased out of bed, gathered up her robe, and went into the living room where she wouldn't disturb him. There was no need for *both* of them to be interrupted by her zany sister.

"Oh! I'll just have to tell you! I can't stand it anymore! I'm in *his* room…at least I think it's him. He's staying the night with a friend, so I got his room!"

"*Whose* room!?" Jo Ann insisted.

"It all fits. This is the part of the state where his adoptive parents were from. And his name's the same—you know the social worker told you she thought they'd kept the name you gave him. And his picture! He looks just like Ellie and Victoria, and he's just the right age! In fact, his parents told me his birthday was yesterday—March 25—and that's the day *he* was born."

Maxine paused for one breathless second and then let it

out as loudly as she dared. "I'm in Brandon's room! I just know it!"

Jo Ann was fully awake now. Her mind was spinning. Was it possible? Could it be true? She shivered at the thought as a chill ran through her body.

He would be seventeen by now. The same age she'd been when she'd had him. When she'd found out she was pregnant, she couldn't bring herself to tell anyone—not even the baby's father. She'd been so scared, so ashamed. But Maxine, who was just sixteen at the time, had guessed. She'd seen the fear in her sister's eyes, and she'd heard her crying in the night. When Jo Ann's secret could be kept no longer, Maxine had coaxed her into telling her boyfriend, and then she'd sat beside Jo Ann as she told their parents. And when the decision was made that Jo Ann would give her baby up for adoption and spend the last three months of her pregnancy at her aunt's home in Delaware, Maxine had insisted on going too. Everyone in their little church and town had thought they were vacationing for the summer— after Jo Ann's senior year. While her friends had taken senior trips to the beach or to Europe, she'd had a baby. And she'd been all alone—except for Maxine.

When the labor pains began, it had been Maxine who

held her hand and whispered soothing memories of happier days. It had been Maxine who helped her cry when they whisked the screaming, red bundle out of the room. It had been Maxine who supported her as they boarded the plane back home—and away from Jo Ann's son. And it had been Maxine who made her feel like a normal teenager again as they sat together on the bed and giggled about innocent, girlish things.

And now her sister's voice flew through the telephone wires, bristling with excitement. "It's him, Jo Ann; I just know it is!"

When Jo Ann hung up the phone, her mind whirled through all the possibilities. She'd always hoped that when Brandon turned eighteen, he would want to meet her and John. After several years of wild living, she and John had settled down and actually gotten married. Their love for each other had matured and ripened, and they had both returned to the Christian values they'd been raised with.

Not a day passed that she didn't think about where their son might be, that she didn't wonder what he looked like and if he were happy, that she didn't long to know him…to hold him in her arms.

After hearing Maxine's news, Jo Ann's first instinct was

to jump in her car, drive to the airport, and fly to his house. But she knew she couldn't. She'd often dreamed of finding her son, but she was of the full conviction that it would be wrong to disrupt his life—and the lives of the adoptive parents who'd loved him and raised him all these years—by trying to contact him before he was eighteen. And even then, it would be up to Brandon to decide if he wanted to meet them. She knew he might not.

It didn't take long for Maxine and Jo Ann to find the social worker who'd placed Brandon those many years ago. Then came the seemingly endless wait until Brandon neared his eighteenth birthday. Just a few weeks before his birthday, the social worker made contact with Brandon and his family and let them know that his biological parents had ended up getting married and wanted very much to meet him…if he wanted to.

But Brandon had no desire to meet the parents who'd given him up. Crushed, Jo Ann tried to lay her dream aside, but the ache in her heart grew with each passing day.

Then, just four days before Brandon's nineteenth birthday, the social worker called to say that Brandon wanted to meet his biological sisters. He had no sisters in his adoptive family, and the idea that he had two sisters whom he'd never met intrigued him.

As Jo Ann stood nervously at the window—straining to see down the driveway, waiting for some sign of movement—Maxine quietly slipped up beside her and took Jo Ann's quivering hand. She could see Ellie and Victoria in the front-porch swing, talking excitedly as they anxiously waited to meet their brother for the first time. The close relationship of the teenage sisters reminded Jo Ann of her love for Maxine.

After ten more agonizing minutes, a blue Toyota turned slowly into the driveway. Jo Ann and Maxine stood transfixed, watching the two curly haired girls race to meet the car. As they neared the car, Victoria and Ellie slowed their pace and tried to recapture their composure.

Jo Ann held her breath as the tall, handsome young man stepped out of the car. The resemblance was astonishing. The same light-brown, curly hair, the same tall, lean body. The three faces beamed with identical smiles. After a few hesitant words were exchanged, the two sisters took their newfound brother by the hand and led him toward the house—and their mother.

With just a few smooth strides of their long legs, the trio stood before her.

"Brandon," Jo Ann said almost timidly, "I'm Jo Ann, your biological mother, and this is your Aunt Maxine—she was there when you were born."

The minutes before his arrival had seemed like hours; now time stood still as Jo Ann awaited his response. Their eyes locked together—mother and son. Neither one of them moved.

And then Brandon's eyes softened, and a broad smile spread across his face. Letting go of his sisters' hands, he engulfed the two older sisters in a warm embrace and said, "I look forward to getting to know you—all of you."

As Brandon stepped back, Jo Ann felt the gentle squeeze of her sister's hand and knew that her life had now come full circle—and her sister had been there every step of the way.

5

a Sister's
challenge

*W*hen you are pure in heart,
you'll receive blessings and see Me.
Prevent sin by hiding Scripture in
your heart and living according to My
Word. I'll give you a pure heart and
renew a steadfast spirit within you.

Blessings,
Your Holy God

—from Matthew 5:8; Psalms 119:9; 51:10

Sisters

A sister can be pretty demanding. When you were little, she may have demanded to have your doll or her way or your mom's attention. But sometimes, now that you're adults, she might demand something else: She might demand that you be all God has called you to be. And that's a good kind of demand—rising from a love that settles only for the best in you.

And there may have been a time—or a time may yet come—when your sister had to come to your rescue, a time when she had to rescue you from yourself. A time when you'd lost sight of who you are in God and were swept away by something that, deep down, you knew was not who you really are. It may have been a spirit of bitterness toward your husband or a heart full of fear about the future or a lustful attraction for someone who was not yours to have.

Not many have earned the right to challenge you at times like these. Not many have invested years of being there for you, hours of listening to your hurts, or a lifetime of getting to know you. But a sister has. A sister has earned the right to "urge you to live a life worthy of the calling you have received" (Ephesians 4:1).

A sister has earned the right to take you by the shoulders, look you in the eyes, and say what needs to be said. She's tough all right. But a sister who calls you to a "life worthy of the calling" also knows how to restore her sister with gentleness and love.

Sisters settle only for the best that each can be.

For there is no friend like a sister,
In calm or stormy weather,
To cheer one on the tedious way,
To fetch one if one goes astray,
To lift one if one totters down,
To strengthen whilst one stands.

—Christina Rossetti

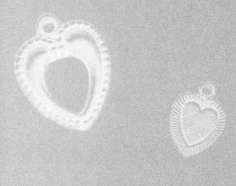

On the outside,
everything
appeared
unchanged. But on
the inside, she was
a tangled mass of
emotions.

only the best

Georgia stole a furtive glance at Mark from across the room. His eyes caught hers, and they exchanged a look full of secrecy and longing. Georgia felt a flush rise to her face. She looked away quickly and hoped that none of their coworkers had noticed.

The director of the marketing department sat at the head of the large, mahogany table and was saying something about the ad campaign that she and Mark were working on together. She tried to concentrate. But her thoughts kept drifting back to last night.

The spark between them had first ignited one night when they were working late. They'd been standing over the drafting table. Mark had teased Georgia about something, and she had playfully placed her hand on his chest to push him away. She felt the electricity between them immediately. He had quickly put his hand over hers before she'd had a chance to remove it and had looked meaningfully into her eyes. He'd released his hold shortly, and they had gone back to work, but their relationship was forever changed.

Each time they were alone together after that night, the heat between them intensified. Their conversations had gone from flirtatious to suggestive to tantalizing. They'd moved from playful touches to tender caresses.

Last night had been electric. A slight smile spread across Georgia's lips as she relived the scene in her mind.

"Georgia." It was her director, Chris. "Georgia, tell us about the campaign you and Mark have been working on the past couple of weeks. Don't think I haven't noticed how hard you two have been working on this project. You've put a lot of overtime in on this one. I have every confidence that you're going to impress us."

Georgia stuttered and stammered, trying to compose her thoughts. Mark saw her predicament and rescued her. He took over the conversation and laid out their plan with polished ease and tasteful flamboyance. He was the kind of man who could think fast on his feet and charm anyone—like he'd charmed her.

The intensity of the desire Georgia felt for Mark surprised her. She had never wanted something she wasn't supposed to have more than she wanted Mark. It wasn't that she was unhappy in her marriage. She loved her husband very much. She was devoted to her three children. It was the thrill of being wanted. The excitement of being pursued. Mark had awakened sensuous emotions in her that had lain dormant for years.

But for all the exhilaration of their clandestine relationship, Georgia could never completely rid herself of the nagging guilt. She had always been a strong Christian. She had been raised by Christian parents. She and her husband and children went to church three times a week. In the past, when she'd heard of someone cheating on his or her spouse, she'd been bewildered. Even judgmental. How could people do that? Did they have no standards? No convictions?

And now, here she was. But surely this was different. She wasn't out to take Mark away from his wife. She definitely had no plans to leave her own family. This was just some innocent fun. Some harmless flirtation. She had the situation under control. She knew where to draw the line. As

Georgia relived the excitement of the night before, she tried not to think about how close she had come to stepping over that line.

They had worked late again—and alone. When they'd begun to run out of excuses to stay, Mark had abandoned all pretense and taken her in his muscular arms. He had spoken tenderly and provocatively of his desire for her. Georgia's body had melted into his. As he smiled down upon her, Georgia traced his lips with her finger. He drew her closer, and when their lips met, the last bit of Georgia's reserve dissolved. If the night janitor had not accidentally announced his coming by knocking over a trash can, nothing would have restrained her.

Georgia was jolted out of her musings as everyone around her rose to their feet. The meeting was over. She had no idea what it had been about. She was careful not to walk out with Mark. She spoke cordially to a couple of her colleagues as they walked down the hall together. She kept her gaze neutral as she watched Mark round the corner to his office.

Georgia felt certain that no one suspected their secret romance. She refrained from talking about Mark with her coworkers. She regulated her facial expression if they met in the hall.

She was surprised at how easy it was to carry on her home life as if nothing out of the ordinary were going on. She still went to church. She still taught the two-year-olds' class she'd taught for five years. On the outside, everything appeared unchanged. But on the inside, she was a tangled mass of emotions.

The intercom on her phone beeped. She picked up the receiver.

"Hi." Mark's voice was rich with undertones. "I'm thirsty. Meet me in the break room."

Georgia felt her heart quicken. She took a deep breath, and her chest filled with warm expectancy. But with the next breath came an uneasiness that threatened to dampen her passion. Something was vexing her heart—an uncertainty, an unsettling confusion. She was losing the sense of who she was. She used to be so sure. She used to know exactly who she was and Whom she belonged to. Now her identity was getting fuzzy. Lines that were once definitive and concrete had become obscure and vague. Georgia consciously squelched the disquietude in her heart. Within seconds, she could feel her reason shutting down and her emotions taking over. Those bothersome voices were finally silenced.

She tried not to hurry as she walked down the hall.

Her breath came faster and faster as she neared the break room. She willed herself to slow down, gathering her scattered composure as she entered the room.

He was leaning up against the Coke machine. His Armani suit fit his trim body perfectly. He was smiling that gorgeous smile. "I was just dying for something to quench my thirst. I had to have a look at *you*." His words dripped seduction.

It was happening again. She was turning to butter. Willless, mindless, melting butter. She was so absorbed in the vision of him that she didn't hear the footsteps behind her. But she was awakened from her dream-state by the voice.

"Hey, sis. I've been looking all over for you. Did you forget our lunch date?"

It was her sister LinDee.

LinDee took a tentative step forward and moved between Mark and Georgia, intuitively assessing the tension in the room. Then she fixed her gaze steadily on her sister. "Are you ready?"

"Ah…sure," Georgia faltered. "I was just…uh… thirsty…"

Georgia's eyes unintentionally locked onto Mark's. His lips curled in a half-smile, and his eyes tried to disguise a mischievous twinkle.

None of it was lost on LinDee.

LinDee took Georgia by the arm and deliberately guided her out of the room. They walked in silence down the hall and into the elevator.

"What was *that* all about?" LinDee blurted as soon as the door closed and the elevator bell signaled its descent. LinDee was not one to mince words.

"What do you mean?" Georgia mustered all the innocence she could.

"You know good and well what I mean. I mean what's going on between you and that guy?"

"Oh, LinDee, you're just imagining things. You know how you let your imagination run away with you sometimes."

"And you know how you let your emotions run away with you sometimes. We'll talk about it later."

Georgia breathed a sigh of relief. She knew how easily her sister was distracted. She'd probably forget all about it before they sat down to eat. "Where should we go?" Georgia asked with deliberate cheerfulness.

"I've already got it figured out," LinDee replied. "I reserved a cozy corner table at a new Italian restaurant that Jim and I tried out last week. It's just a couple of blocks from here. We can walk. How does that sound?"

"Great by me."

Heads turned as the two women walked briskly down the street, arm in arm. The crisp fall temperatures brought a blush to their cheeks, and the clear sunlight brought out the shine in their brown hair. They talked intimately about their kids and their jobs and their latest projects.

People often said they looked like twins except for their eyes. LinDee's blue eyes flashed with strength and deliberation, while Georgia's soft, brown eyes were gentle and full of emotion. Both women had an unaffected, natural beauty that seemed to draw others to them.

After they'd ordered, the two sisters settled comfortably into their chairs. Soothing Italian music played in the background, muting the conversation of the few other patrons who were there. It was almost as if they had the restaurant to themselves.

LinDee set her tea glass down and fixed her eyes on

Georgia's, looking deep into them. "Okay, Georgia. Give. I know something is going on between you and that guy—I can feel it in my bones—and if it's what I think it is, then I also know it's not what you really want. It's not who you really are."

LinDee's challenge caught Georgia off guard.

"You've got it all wrong," Georgia protested weakly, trying to maintain eye contact. But it was no use. She couldn't look into her sister's penetrating gaze and lie at the same time. She had to look away.

LinDee's magnetic stare forced Georgia's eyes back to hers.

"No, I don't think I have it all wrong. I think I've got it exactly right." LinDee leaned across the table and gently caressed Georgia's trembling hand. "Georgia, you are my sister. But more importantly, you are a precious child of God. Your whole identity is wrapped up in Him. I know without a doubt that deep in your heart you don't want to throw away what you've believed your whole life. Because, Georgia, you can't have it both ways. You can't have this impure relationship and your heavenly Father too. You know that, don't you, sis?"

It seemed that in an instant Georgia's pretense was

unveiled. Her heart was melted. But this was a holy kind of melt, not the kind she felt with Mark. Her spirit immediately recognized the difference—now that her heart had been opened to the truth by her precious sister.

Tears welled up in Georgia's eyes, and she felt a purity of heart she hadn't felt in weeks. The cobwebs that had confused her mind were cleared away. The truth was so obvious now. How had she not seen it before?

Somehow, she knew what she had to do. Her boss had recently offered her a promotion that would move her to an office across town. Immediately she knew she would take it. She wasn't sure her resolve could hold if she had to see Mark every day.

Georgia now looked willingly into LinDee's compassionate eyes. As powerful as the attraction was between her and Mark, the bond she shared with her sister was empowered with a heavenly force. Georgia squeezed LinDee's hand affectionately.

Since they were little girls sitting around the dinner table, the squeezing of hands had always precipitated prayer. Simultaneously, the two women bowed their heads.

Georgia's heart burst open as she found herself face to face with her heavenly Father. "Dear God, please forgive me for betraying who I am in You. Forgive me for deluding myself with a lie. Thank you so much for using my sister to show me the truth and break down the walls of my self-deception. I place my heart in your hands."

Georgia opened her eyes and extended her other hand to her sister.

"Thank you for reminding me of who I am and Whom I belong to. I can always count on you to rescue me—even when you have to rescue me from myself."

"Just like I can count on you," LinDee said sweetly. "Remember the time…"

The love between these two women was the kind of love that refused to leave things alone—the kind of love that said the tough stuff, that hung on during the storm, that settled only for the best that each could be.

6

a Sister's
service

$\mathcal{U}$se the gifts I've given you to serve others. Make love your motivation. I stockpile you with My all-sufficient grace, equipping you with more than enough for every good deed I've prepared for you.

Serve Joyfully,
Jesus

—from 1 Peter 4:10; 1 Corinthians 16:14;
2 Corinthians 9:8

Sisters

"Be nice to your sister!"

Sound familiar? With just a little bit of concentration, you can probably hear your mother's voice echoing back from...well, we won't say *how* many years...but from somewhere in the "not-too-distant" past.

Did you ever get tired of trying to be nice to your sister? Maybe, even now, she taxes your patience on occasion. Like when she tries to tell you how to raise your kids before she's even raised hers. Or when she is at your house as a guest and insists on setting the table her way. You have to admit: As much as you love her, you sometimes get tired of being nice to your sister.

But there are times when she *really* needs you. And sometimes the need goes on for longer than is comfortable. It's at times like these that we can be spurred on only by some other words from the distant past, but these words carry even more authority than your mother's: "Let us not become weary of doing good, for at the proper time we will reap a harvest if we do not give up" (Galatians 6:9).

Something about those words infuses the weary heart with strength and the ability to keep going: It's the acknowledgment of the fact that doing good *is* wearisome at times. And that acknowledgment allows us to feel that we're not alone in our weariness and to know that it's a trait common to all people—even sisters who are trying to serve but are tired of trying. And that acknowledgment—coupled with the godly reminder to persevere and the promise of future reward—gives us the strength and the resolve to keep on being nice to our sisters.

Grant also that even in the guise of the fretful, the demanding, the unreasonable, I may still recognize You and say: My suffering Jesus, how sweet it is to serve You.

—Mother Teresa

Today was going to
be a good day, and
she was going to keep
her cool no matter
how many times that
buzzer clanged.

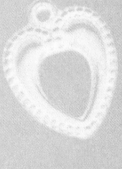

we shall not be moved

The intruding buzz jolted Ellen from her concentration. With one swift, automatic motion, she pressed the "save" keys on her keyboard and pushed herself up from the cherry wood desk. She had vowed the night before, as she prayed for strength, that she would be patient today...that she would "count it all joy" to serve her aging sister.

This was the first "buzz" of the day, and she felt ready. With resolute, cheerful steps, she walked down the two flights of stairs to her sister's room.

"Ellen, could you adjust the fan? I'm chilled all the way to my bones and can't seem to get warm." Flora seemed to get smaller every month. It wasn't just her weight that was dropping, but the space between the bottom of her feet and the foot of the bed was noticeably longer than it had been just two months earlier. And her skin was so wrinkled. There was way too much of it for her bones. But in spite of her slight, weakened frame, there was a lot of life left in Flora. It still sparkled from her crisp, blue eyes that crinkled when she smiled. And there was a lot of love left in her too.

Flora hated to disturb her sister. She knew that the book Ellen was writing was due in just two weeks. She'd waited as long as she could before calling, but if she didn't get warm, the dreaded shivers would begin. When they started, she just couldn't stop them. Her teeth would begin to chatter, and her whole body would shake. And sometimes, that set off the spasms in her legs. When they took hold of her, she would be overcome with panic and such a sense of helplessness.

"There you go," Ellen said tenderly. "Is that better?"

"Just right. Thank you, Ellen. I'll try not to call you again for a while."

"That's all right, sis. Call me whenever you need me. The exercise is good for me."

As Ellen walked back up the stairs, her thoughts returned to the novel she was working on. It was the third one in the series. She had introduced a new character in the last chapter and was having a hard time getting into his head. If she could have just one hour of uninterrupted thought, she could get it all figured out.

She grabbed a Diet Coke out of the refrigerator she kept in her study and sat back down at her computer. Ever since her husband died three years earlier, she had struggled with her writing. There was something about his easygoing humor and self-assured gentleness that had set her mind at ease and freed it up to think and create. Her mind was never completely at ease now. If she wasn't fretting about her sister, she was worrying about her daughter in London at law school or her son studying photography in Baton Rouge. She felt the weight of it all; there was no one to help her carry the load. And if she didn't get this book written, she'd have no money to pay the bills. It was all up to her. Sometimes she didn't know if she could do it.

But today, she felt strong. Today was going to be a good day, and she was going to keep her cool no matter how many times that buzzer clanged.

Ellen set herself to the task before her. And before she knew it, her fingers were flying around the keyboard and a story line was appearing on her screen. She was beginning to like this new character. She looked a bit like herself, a "youthful" forty-nine-year-old with shoulder-length, slightly graying hair and a trim five-foot-five frame.

Just a few more pages, and she'd have this scene worked out.

Buzzz! Ellen had bought the buzzer for Flora when she'd first moved in. The third-floor room that had become Ellen's office was some distance from Flora, but it was the only room that would accommodate the roll-top desk she had inherited from their grandmother and give her a view of the lake behind her sister's house. Ellen had always been drawn to the water. She didn't particularly like being *in* the water, but she loved being *near* it. She'd spent countless, unmeasured hours walking along the lake's edge during the months after Phil had died. Nothing could soothe her tormented spirit like a breeze blowing across the lake and across her face. And so she'd chosen this isolated room in order to see the lake. And that's why she'd installed the buzzer. All Flora had to do was push a button, and Ellen would know she was needed.

And Flora never called Ellen unless she really needed her. Ellen knew that it pained Flora to have to depend on her younger sister for her every need. With predetermined cheerfulness, Ellen left her story and pointed her feet toward the stairs.

"What ya need, sis?" Her sweetness wasn't forced. Ellen dearly loved her ailing sister and wanted her to be as comfortable as possible. Flora had been plagued with illnesses of all sorts since childhood. She'd had nine surgeries and had been in the hospital with pneumonia so many times that Ellen had lost count. The most difficult problem lately was the unexplained spasms that would inevitably cause Flora's lower body to go absolutely stiff. It seemed that any number of things could set them off. The only thing that seemed to help was a vigorous, long massage.

"I've misplaced my pen and writing pad, and I wanted to write a letter to Joshua." Joshua was Flora's youngest grandchild. He had surprised the whole family two weeks earlier by walking out on his wife of six years and their two small children. "He's so mixed up and confused right now, and so much of the family has turned against him. I can't understand how he could leave his babies and that sweet Janene, but even though he's totally in the wrong, God has put it on my heart to write him and let him know that I love him. I pray for him every day; I'd climb out of bed right now and get down on my knees for him if this body would let me."

"Here it is, Flora, right here in your nightstand drawer."

"Oh, dear. I'm so sorry. I don't know how I missed it. Thank you, Ellen. You're such a love."

"No problem, sweetie. You know how to call me if you need me again."

And Flora did need her. The rest of the morning was interrupted frequently with opportunities for "exercise" and "joyful service." It seemed that every time Ellen got a thought going, the buzzer would sound. But with each intrusion, she uttered a quick prayer for resolve and determined to be sweet—and mean it. Maybe the afternoon would be less demanding.

But when the downstairs grandfather clock struck four at the same time as the buzzer snarled for the hundredth time, Ellen's resolve began to unravel. She'd written only four pages all day. And she had two hundred to go.

As she marched down the stairs, her footsteps were heavy and loud. She forced a smile to her face as she entered Flora's room. "What is it, dear?" she asked through almost clenched teeth.

"I'm afraid I've made a terrible mess," Flora lamented. "I spilled orange juice all over myself."

This was going to require some major time. She might as

well give up for the day. "Let's get you out of bed, and I'll change your sheets," Ellen said, trying to keep the irritation out of her voice. "I'll go get your wheelchair."

Ellen was gone only moments, but when she came back into the room, Flora's face was contorted and her legs were convulsing in violent spasms. Ellen hurried to her bedside. She quickly pulled back the covers and began to firmly massage her sister's shaking legs. But they were already beginning to stiffen. In a matter of seconds, they were completely rigid.

Ellen struggled with her sister's resistant legs, trying to coax the knees to bend so she could get her into the wheelchair, but they stubbornly refused. At that moment every bit of Ellen's determination disappeared. She turned to the wall so her sister couldn't see her face, and without meaning to, she let out an exasperated scream.

She wasn't mad at her sister. She was mad at the situation. She was mad at life. She was mad about the pain and sickness that her sister had to endure. She was mad at Phil for dying and leaving her alone, and mad at her children for growing up. She was mad at the deadline that forced an undeveloped story from her mind.

When she turned to face her responsibility, she saw the

tears in her sister's eyes. Her heart was filled with instant remorse and compassion.

"I'm so sorry, Flora. It's not you I'm mad at. It's just that I'm tired and my story won't come together and I miss Phil and…"

As her words spilled over one another in an effort to explain, the tears in her sister's eyes took on an odd twinkle. Flora began pumping her arms vigorously. She looked down at her stiffened legs, and in a shaky, little voice, began to sing a song they'd sung years before in the old country church where they'd grown up, "—We shall not be moved."

Surprise, then relief, then joyful release flooded Ellen's heart. She sank down in the wheelchair and began to chuckle as her sister sang on: "Tho all hell assail us, we shall not be moved. Tho the tempest rages, we shall not be moved. Just like a tree that's planted by the wa-a-a-ters, we shall not be moved!"

By the song's end, Ellen was laughing so hard that tears were rolling down her face. And Flora giggled until her whole body began to shake all over again. But this time, it was not from painful spasms, but with childlike joy.

When their laughter subsided, Ellen took her sister's dry, wrinkled hand in her own. "I really do love living here and being with you. You know that, don't you, Flora? I may get frustrated at times, but it's not at you; it's just at life."

Ellen saw nothing but understanding and love in her sister's eyes.

"Come on," Ellen said. "Let me work that stiffness out of your legs, and we'll get you in your wheelchair and go for a walk down by the lake."

Minutes later, two well-seasoned sisters could be seen by the lake's edge, the younger pushing the older in a wheelchair. And with renewed resolve and refreshed commitment, they sang loud and clear, "Just like a tree that's planted by the wa-a-a-ters, we shall not be moved."

7

a *Sister's*
memories

$\mathcal{L}$ook to Me. Remember the days of old;

consider all the wonderful things I've done

for you. Remember things that are noble,

pure, and right. Reflect on everything

that is praiseworthy or excellent!

Love,

Your God of History

—from Deuteronomy 32:7; Psalm 105:4–5;

Philippians 4:8

Sisters

Remember the time…

Sisters share memories that define who they are—memories that date back to their very beginnings.

Remember the time you told her the secret that had been haunting you, and she understood? Remember the time you laughed till you cried over something that wasn't really all that funny? Remember the time she hurt your feelings and said she was sorry? Remember the time you hurt hers? Remember the time you needed her and she was there? Remember the time you giggled together about the new boy who'd moved in next-door? Remember the time you did something your mother had told you not to do and your sister told on you? Remember the time she didn't?

Memories make us

who we are, and memories of our sisters
are tucked deep inside of us in places we may
not often visit but that shape our very core.

"Remember the days of old," Moses told
the Israelites (Deuteronomy 32:7). He knew that
in the remembering, they would reconnect with
who they were and Whom they belonged to.

Memories connect us with our past and
with our future. They give us a sense of where we
fit in the scheme of things; they help us feel
rooted and steady in a perplexing world.

Go ahead. Pick up the phone. Call
your sister. Ask her how the kids are doing
or what's new on the job, and then ask
her if she remembers the time…

You'll both be filled with
a renewed sense of who you
are and who you want
to be.

How could we endure to live and let time pass if we were always crying for one day or one year to come back—if we did not know that every day in a life fills the whole life with expectation and memory and that these are that day.

—*Out of the Silent Planet*, C. S. Lewis

*If anyone knew about
remembering, it was
these three sisters.*

pleasure full grown

Nina lay the open book facedown in her lap. As she leaned her head against the back of the old rocking chair, she closed her eyes and let out a dreamy sigh.

"I wonder if it's true…"

She opened her clear, blue eyes and looked across the room at her older sister Mattye Lou, who was crocheting a yellow blanket for her soon-to-be-born eleventh grandchild.

"You wonder if what's true, Nina? You're forever starting conversations in the middle instead of where they begin. Whatever are you talking about?"

"I wonder if it's true that 'a pleasure is full grown only when it is remembered.'"

Pearl, Nina's younger sister, stood her iron on the ironing board and put her hands on her hips. "Now what in the world is that supposed to mean? Are you reading one of those sappy romance novels again?"

"I am not." Nina tried to sound offended, but the sparkle in her eyes communicated more affection than offense. "I'm reading C. S. Lewis, I'll have you know. And I've come across the most wonderful passage. The main character of the book is a space traveler, and he's having a conversation with a creature from another planet about the pleasure of lovemaking."

"Land sakes alive, Nina! You are too reading a sappy romance novel," Pearl insisted.

"No, no," Mattye Lou interrupted. "C. S. Lewis is a Christian writer, but I still have no idea what our batty sister is talking about."

"Well, if you'll be quiet and listen, I'll tell you. An earth man is talking with a creature from another planet, and the earth man just can't comprehend why these creatures make love to their mates only while they are young. Now listen to what the creature says about the males of his species." Nina lifted the book so she could read it more easily. "'But it'—" Nina peered over the top of the book and looked authoritatively at her sisters. She had her "teacher" expression on. "By 'it,' he means not 'lovemaking,' but 'love,'" she explained. Nina had spent most of her adult life as an elementary school teacher, and to the chagrin of her sisters, she frequently slipped back into that role. When she was satisfied that they were paying attention and had grasped her meaning, she turned her eyes to the page once again.

"'But it takes his whole life. When he is young he has to look for his mate; and then he has to court her; then he begets young; then he rears them; then he remembers all this, and boils it inside him and makes it into poems and wisdom.'"

Nina's voice slowed its pace and filled with emotion as she read the parts about *remembering* and *boiling* and *poems* and *wisdom*.

"Here's where Hyoi, the space creature, says it," Nina voice was wistful and breathy: "'A pleasure is full grown only when it is remembered.'"

Nina closed the book, laid it on her lap, and ceremoniously folded her hands upon it, as if she had just spoken the final word in some matter of great importance. Sweet expressions of understanding had replaced the incredulity that had played across her sisters' faces when she'd begun her reading. She put the question to them again: "Do you think it's true? Do you think it's true that part of the pleasure of life's events is in the *remembering?*"

If anyone knew about remembering, it was these three sisters. Mattye Lou, the eldest, would be eighty-one next month. Nina was three years younger, and Pearl, "the baby," had just celebrated her seventy-fifth. Their children, long raised, had children of their own—some even had grandchildren. Between them, the sisters had survived two floods, one bankruptcy, the divorces of two children, a seven-year battle with breast cancer, and the deaths of six husbands—Nina holding the record with three. They were sturdy women, from hearty stock. Strong of character, strong on conviction, and strong in their faith. Yes, if anyone could judge the truth of Hyoi's statement, they could.

"Well," Mattye Lou mused, "I remember the time Jack and I went sailing in the San Diego bay one day in June. We'd only been married two weeks, and we didn't have a care in the world. It was the most beautiful day—you know how I relish a beautiful day. I remember lifting my face to the sun—I remember taking a deep breath and feeling the salty air fill my lungs—I remember the wind on my face…"

Mattye Lou's voice trailed off, and her blissful expression melted into sadness. "And I remember that only two days later, Jack was killed in that ridiculous airplane. He never was satisfied keeping his feet on the ground. He just had to try to learn to fly. Well, he didn't.

"And that's when you flew out to see me." She turned to look Nina full in the face. "You were so afraid of flying—especially after Jack's accident—but you insisted on coming to be with me. If it hadn't been for you, I don't think I would have survived."

Pearl left her ironing and sat beside Mattye Lou on the worn Victorian couch that graced the middle of the sitting room. "And I remember when I was pregnant with Jordan—my first." Pearl placed both hands on her tummy and sighed with the memory.

"Feeling the movement of that little life for the first time was more thrilling than the day I graduated from medical school. And when my time came, you were right there, Mattye Lou. I'll never forget the look on your face when the nurse tried to tell you that no one was allowed in the labor room except hospital personnel. You shook your finger in her face and told her that your baby sister was not going to go through the horrors of labor alone. All your talk of the 'horrors' of labor scared me to death, but once you were by my side, holding my hand, I knew everything would be okay. And it was."

Nina looked lovingly at her two sisters. If you'd asked her five years ago where she would be now, she would never have guessed that the three of them would be living together in the old family home. These walls echoed memories—memories of childhood, family gatherings, weddings, special meals, births, even deaths—the stuff life is made of. She remembered the good times and the bad. The multi-colored threads of their lives had woven together to create a vibrant tapestry, rich in depth and meaning and passion.

Nina got up from her rocking chair and wedged herself between her sisters on the couch. "Do you remember the time—I think you were about five, Pearl—when Mattye Lou convinced you that if you put your head between the stair banisters, closed your eyes, and counted to a hundred, you would turn into Cinderella?"

Mattye Lou put her hand to her mouth and giggled like a little girl.

"And when your head got stuck," Nina continued,

"Mattye Lou and I got on each side of you, took hold of a rail, and pulled with all our might."

"Yes," Pearl broke in excitedly, "and when both banisters broke at the same time, we all three fell over the railing and tumbled to the floor."

"And when Mother came in and asked what had happened, do you remember what we said?" Nina prodded.

There was a brief moment of recollection, and then, as if on some unspoken command, the three gray-headed sisters rose staunchly to their feet, clasped hands, and turned to face the old staircase behind them. Taking a deep breath, in unison, they recited,

"Sisters forever,

Sisters for real,

True sisters never

Ever will squeal."

You'd think they'd uttered the funniest words ever as they abandoned all decorum and howled with laughter and delight.

Three sisters, bound by blood, bound by their pasts, now sharing their last years. Like the woman in Proverbs 31, they'd lived their lives with dignity and strength. They had provided food for their families, they had made their arms strong with vigorous work, they had loved their husbands, and they had most definitely laughed at the future.

And now, together, they found *pleasure full grown* in remembering days gone by.